BURBANK FEB 12 '62

FEB 1 0 1995

Obert, Karl.
This is California :
photographs /
1958.
33305210598292
cu   05/04/15

THIS IS
CALIFORNIA

PHOTOGRAPHS BY

KARL OBERT
A. P. S. A.   A. R. P. S.

PRINTED IN GERMANY BY

LUDWIG SIMON VERLAG

PUBLISHED IN THE UNITED STATES BY

LANE PUBLISHING CO., MENLO PARK, CALIFORNIA
Publishers of Sunset Magazine and Books

Santa Clara County Free Library
San Jose, Calif.

336573

Library of Congress Catalog Card Number: 57-8517

Published in the United States by Lane Publishing Co.

Printed in Germany

Published in Germany by Ludwig Simon, Munich-Pullach

Production: R. Oldenbourg, Graphische Betriebe GmbH, Munich

1957

First Edition 15,000

Santa Clara County Free Library
San Jose, Calif.

F 917.94
O12

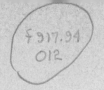

Foreword

In arranging and compiling this book about California, I started from San Diego, the southern-most tip jutting into the Pacific, followed the "path of the Padres" along the coast—*El Camino Real*—The Mission Trail, going from city to city and into the valleys along the coast, all the way to the Oregon border, then turning, and crossing inland to view Mt. Shasta, and Mt. Lassen. Progressing south down the Great Central Valley, stopping at Sacramento, the Capital, turning to the western foothills of the Sierra, and coming southward into Yosemite and Sequoia National Parks, traveling through Mojave Desert and into the San Bernardino Mountains, for by this time we are back in Southern California.

Coming down the south slopes of the San Bernardino Mountains, we enter the desert near Palm Springs, going all the way to the Salton Sea, turning north we travel to the eastern slopes of the Sierra, and Red Rock Canyon. From there we head deep into Death Valley which contains the lowest point in the United States (282 feet below sea level). Only a few miles away we reach the Sierra and come to Mt. Whitney, the highest point in this country (14,495 feet).

We follow the eastern edge of the Sierra, proceed northward, making many side trips into the beautiful lake areas of the High Sierra, and venturing up several of the various mountain passes in the region. Then into the high desert country we visit the Ghost Town of Bodie, once a famous old mining camp. Going up to beautiful Lake Tahoe, we proceed to peaceful Donner Lake, then from there, up historic Donner Pass.

This encompasses and includes man's and nature's handiwork which makes California one of the most beautiful states in the Union.

Karl Obert
A. P. S. A.   A. R. P. S.

336573

Introduction

"California" began as a dream in the mind of the Spanish writer, Garcia Ordóñez de Montalvo, soon after Columbus discovered the New World. His fanciful novel, which was widely read around 1510, told of a mythical island "at the right hand of the Indies" called "California". Dreams of the Indies and gold were driving Europeans westward across the Atlantic, leading them into strange new places from which they sent home exaggerated reports based upon poor observations, wrong information from Indians, false calculations—and their own dreams of what they wanted to find. Early explorers pushing across the wilds of Mexico encountered the 700-mile-long Gulf of California (Sea of Cortez) and concluded that the land across the gulf was a great island, rather than a peninsula. It better fitted their plans that it should be an island, since the Spanish explorers were looking for the "Strait of Anian" and Drake sought the same thing as "Northwest Passage" — a water route to the Indies, the goal of their dreams.

Borrowing from the "best seller" of their day, they named what they found "California" and showed it on their maps as an island for the next hundred years.

California has remained a land of dreams for millions—sleepy dreams for the Spanish and Mexicans who did little with it for more than two centuries; challenging dreams for the Englishmen Drake and Vancouver who wanted only to find a way past it; commercial dreams for the Russians who used it as a base for their fur-seeking operations farther north; exciting "manifest destiny" dreams for the Americans pushing westward across their continent; wild, maddening dreams for men all over the world who in 1849 rushed to California for the gold the Spanish had ignored.

Since dreams have a most personal quality, they vary greatly from person to person. The 8 million visitors to California every year probably take home 8 million different memories; the legions planning a first trip undoubtedly enjoy greatly differing ideas of what they will find; the more than 13 million present inhabitants must see their state in nearly as many different ways.

When a fine German photographer named Karl Obert followed his dreams to California, he soon became obsessed with the vision of photographing the state to give others in the world a better idea of what California is today and to provide residents and visitors with a gallery of beautiful pictures. For more than 30 years he has traveled up and down and back and forth over the great expanse of California, training his cameras and discerning eyes upon it, catching the flavor of Spain in old buildings, the glories of nature in the rocky coast, the peaceful valleys, the walls of Yosemite. Small wonder that Ludwig Simon in Germany decided to produce this volume in English, French, and German; that the publishers of *Sunset* Magazine in California bring it to the American public. This is Karl Obert's California, presented in the kind of fine pictures that have won him international fame and membership in both the Associate Photographic Society of America and the Associate Royal Photographic Society of England. Entire volumes can and have been done on single aspects of this kaleidoscopic state. "Scenic California" could not be fully represented by a thousand pictures of the sandy beaches, the rocky coast, the bays and lakes and harbors, the hundreds of large and small valleys, the myriad of mountain peaks, the towering walls, deep shadows, and rushing falls of Yosemite, the soft, rounded hills, the redwood trees. "California at Play" would need to cover the greatest recreational area in the world, including 1200 miles of coastline, thousands of mountain campsites, and rushing trout streams, ski jumps and desert resorts, as well as Disneyland, world-famous golf courses, noted restaurants, and stadiums crowded with a hundred thousand spectators. "California at Work" would range from cowboys on horseback to vast aircraft factories turning out jet planes, and beautiful actresses performing before TV cameras. Each major city contains more than enough for a large book; Los Angeles with its teeming population, San Francisco on its seven hills arching its graceful bridges across the Bay. "Transportation" with its story of railroads, rivers, bays and giant airports would need a thousand varied pictures, as would the story of great libraries, universities and other institutions.

Many books would be required to record fully the hundreds of variations found in the homes and ways of life in modern California, caused partly by the gentle climate that stimulates an abundance of outdoor living around nearly every home; caused mostly by the attitude of its residents, an attitude influenced by everything California is, an attitude that shapes houses and gardens into stimulating designs that have been copied the world over.

California is changing every day as about a thousand people a day cross its borders to become residents, bringing their ideas, building their homes in orchards, valleys and up mountain sides. But they in turn are even more influenced by the climate, the vastness and the centuries of history that have shaped California—overpowering qualities that withstand the onrush of population.

This book shows California as Karl Obert's keen eyes see it today as the joint product of natural forces and millions of humans who have erected its buildings, cultivated its soil, dammed its streams and constructed its great railroads and highways.

Except for the Indians, the first man to set foot on California was probably Rodriguez Cabrillo, the Portuguese navigator, who landed at San Diego in 1542, just fifty years after Columbus had discovered America. He sailed up the entire coast of California, suffered complications from a broken arm, died, and was buried on San Miguel Island, close to Santa Barbara. Thus when California "began" Henry VIII was on the throne of England, Elizabeth I was a 9-year-old girl, Sir Francis Drake was a small boy, and William Penn, Sir Walter Raleigh, and the Pilgrims had not yet been born.

This was an era of exploration, not colonization, and Spain dropped serious interest in California for the next 227 years, until 1769 when the threat of the Russians caused them to send a party under Governor Gaspar de Portolá to establish San Diego and search for Monterey Bay, which had been glowingly described by Vizáino in 1602. Portolá explored all the way to the Golden Gate and discovered the immense bay of San Francisco which had eluded all of the mariners who had sailed past the narrow opening.

By now, when California was finally getting started, the east coast of the continent was quite well developed with cities a century old, the English and French were pushing westward toward the mountains, and the Spanish governments in Madrid and Mexico City were rapidly deteriorating. The decline had begun with the defeat of the Spanish Armada 181 years before, and the days of glory were over for Spain. California was at the end of a tenuous umbilical cord from Mexico City which had little interest in the new infant. It was the priests in search of new souls to save who now entered the picture.

Father Kino, founder of early Jesuit missions in what are now Mexico and Arizona, had ridden overland in 1701 to Baja (lower) California and for once and all proved that this edge of the continent was not an island. Setting up headquarters in Loreto to the south, the Jesuits prepared to carry their missionary work to the Indians in Alta (upper) California. But this dream they were not permitted to realize. Far back in Madrid, Carlos III signed a document that removed all power from them and, in fact, placed them under arrest, confiscated their property and caused them to be removed back to Vera Cruz. The mantle fell to the Franciscan order.

Governor Portolá launched his expedition northward by both sea and land, and the two parties successfully met after much hardship and founded the first city in California, San Diego. This was in 1769.

Portolá's name has gone down in California history in many places illustrated in this book from San Diego to the Golden Gate, and his reputation remains good. But arriving at San Diego with him was a scholarly, cultured man of great courage and zeal who did far more to develop California, who left his mark and name indelibly throughout most of the state.

Padre Junipero Serra, the Franciscan, now got to work on his dream of founding missions one day's horseback ride apart. Before he and his followers were finished, 21 missions stretched from San Diego to Sonoma, 30 miles above San Francisco. Each became a center of a new way of life for the Indians. Each brought the long-delayed but lasting influence of Spanish architecture that still says "California" to many people. The padres deliberately introduced many kinds of flowers and fruit and nut-producing trees. They soon started small irrigation projects around some of their missions and the dry land began to produce crops, forerunners of the vast agricultural production now sustained by man-made rivers hundreds of miles long that carry melted snows from the High Sierra on the eastern border down to the dry but fertile valleys.

The shaping of California was at last under way. Land grants encompassing thousands of acres were eagerly sought from the Crown. Major parts of some of those early grants are still in the hands of the original families, having survived through the transition of Spanish to Mexican to United States sovereignty. A few rancheros appeared in the landscape at wide intervals, but only two or three towns were established. El Camino Real, running as it does today for nearly the full length of the state, widened from a trail to a path to a dusty road with the missions strung along it like beads approximately every 30 miles.

Barely three months before the situation between the English colonists on the east coast of the continent and King George III reached the boiling point of July 4, 1776, an expedition under Juan Bautista de Anza arrived to colonize San Francisco with nearly 250 men, women, and children, and mules, horses, and cattle. In the same year a little town began at the south end of the San Francisco Bay and was called San Jose. And the capital of both Baja and Alta California was moved north from Loreto to Monterey.

California had at last begun to develop under the Spanish after a delay of 234 years. Only 46 years remained before it would become Mexican rather than Spanish; only 22 years beyond that and it would pass into the hands of Americans. Not foreseeing this, the Spaniards began an easy, lazy life in California, grazing myriads of cattle on the unending golden hills, riding their well-equipped horses, doing no ungentlemanly labor that could be handled by Indians. Mexico City was far away; Madrid was even more remote. Anyway, those governments were more interested in other problems most of the time. The isolated colonists began to think of themselves more and more as "Californios." The overstretched cord was weakening. But they had a good and happy life in the comfortable climate.

In the early 1830's, agitation for the restoration of the mission lands to the Indians, who were recognized as holding title to them under Spanish law, led to the downfall of the missions and Indians alike. The Mexican Congress passed a law in 1833 ordering secularization of the missions and transfer of their wealth and property to the Indian neophytes. Governor Figueroa, charged with enforcement of the law, felt that the Indians were unready for such responsibilities, and he launched a scheme to enforce it gradually, limiting secularization at the start to 10 of the 21 missions. Unfortunately, Figueroa died in 1835, and the secularization was completed hastily and with sad consequences. In 1842 the government in Mexico seized the church's Pious Fund; in 1845 Pio Pico completed the removal of all property from the church. The fine work and high ideals of Kino and Serra crashed to the ground—and so eventually did most of the missions, to be restored years later, some by subscription funds, some by the government. The organization and force which had developed California was ended. The Mission Indians fled to the hills or sank to a state of drunken slavery as scheming whites quickly robbed them of their rights.

Land grants now became the colonizing force. The granting of land to encourage settlement was started by Governor Fages, who gave thousands of acres in the vicinity of Los Angeles to three of Portolá's soldiers who wanted to run cattle. By 1823 there were less than 50 grants in all of California; twenty years later, there were more than 700. The area was beginning to grow.

However, the rest of the world was seething with ambition and action while the Californios basked in their sun. Ships of many nations sailed the Pacific, stopping in California bays to load tallow and hides. Stories about this fair land were carried far and wide and started new dreams in the minds of many men.

The Russians, more interested in business than conquest, established a small fur-trading settlement in 1812 on Spanish land north of San Francisco in polite defiance of the Colonial authorities. Unable to force the Russians out of the colony, the Spanish established two missions north of San Francisco Bay to block southward expansion of the intruders. Although the colony failed after several years, it carried on a brisk trade with the Spanish settlements and missions while it lasted. Eventually, its property was sold to John Augustus Sutter, founder of Sacramento. Relics of the Russian occupation may still be viewed at the restored Fort Ross and at Sutter's Fort, Sacramento.

The irresistible force that has drawn men toward the West since the time of recorded history was working its ferment. Inquisitive Englishmen were fanning out across Canada. Restless Americans had long since scaled the first north-south mountain barrier nearly 3,000 miles to the east, were well across the great plains in the middle of the continent, and were wondering what lay beyond. Only two towering mountain ranges and two deserts lay between them and the Californios, who felt deceptively secure because of the natural barriers to the east and the vast expanse of the Pacific to the west.

But time was running out for the Californios, for immigrants were finding their way to this bountiful land. Some came via the ocean. And they were welcome. John Sutter arrived with his vision of a personal empire and his grant from the Mexican government for many thousands of acres far inland near the head of the great, dry valley called San Joaquin. The year was 1841. Brash American fur trappers were already poking their way through passes in the supposedly impregnable Sierra. The Californios continued with their quiet life, staying instinctively near the coast, where the ships brought them life and glamour, and took their stock in trade—tallow and hides. Sometimes they wondered and complained a bit about their easy-going government with its heart and head so far away. But they never fretted; that wasn't their way. Even the change from Spanish to Mexican rule in 1822 had meant little to them.

Although it was all a mistake in 1842 when American Commodore Thomas Jones sailed three warships into Monterey Bay, it did foreshadow events to come. With only a few sleepy soldiers and ancient cannon at his disposal, the Spanish commandant wisely surrendered the capital of California at once. It was given back to him as soon as Jones discovered that the United States was not (yet) at war with Mexico, and everyone joined in a fiesta to celebrate the whole affair.

But Americans had begun to filter into the colony. Jedediah Smith had visited overland in 1826, the Patties in 1828, and Kit Carson in 1830. The stories they took back to the midwest and east stirred men's imagination.

Destiny was again on the move—"Manifest Destiny" was the name of the cloak thrown over ruthless national ambition. Down on the Rio Grande there had been a bit of "trouble." The vast area which is now known as Texas had been lost by Mexico. James K. Polk became president of the United States. Trouble was coming to California—fast.

Overambitious, enigmatic Captain John Charles Frémont arrived with his "scientific exploration" party in late 1844 and two years later began causing as much trouble with his boastful statements as his rough mountain men did with their crude actions. He soon had the Californios actually taking up arms, but nothing much happened until the Americans wandered to Sonoma, the northernmost town of any importance. Here in a comic, brandy-fired "Revolution" they arrested Don Vallejo and created the "Republic of California" which lasted for 25 days. But the Bear Flag which they hoisted somehow was remembered later and became the official flag when the true state was finally created. When it became known in July that the United States and Mexico were at war after all, Frémont headed south to face the enemy and join General Stephen Kearny who was marching through the southwest with his Army of the West and with orders to take command of the U. S. forces in California. Futile skirmishes, crazy mistakes, and battles in which not a shot was fired now took place—and Frémont took all of California to, and including, San Diego. Unfortunately for Kearny, it was his army of 100 tired and unprepared men who ran into the only major opposition, and suffered 19 killed and 17 wounded in the Battle of San Pasqual. It all ended in Los Angeles on January 13, 1847, when the Californians found themselves caught in a three-way attack by soldiers under Kearny and Frémont and naval forces under Commodore Stockton. General Pico, in command of the native force, chose to surrender to Frémont.

California had become a part of the United States—almost. After military control, a constitutional convention was held and an election followed in November of 1849. But back in Washington the concern was entirely over whether California should be "slave" or "free." Clay, Calhoun, and Webster —giants in debate— joined battle on the issue. California remained without status. For a time three legal codes were in effect simultaneously: military law, Spanish law, and American civil law. It was during this period that many old California families lost their land grants.

Right at this point in her history California reeled under one of the greatest shocks ever to hit any part of the world—GOLD! Within twelve months more people poured into California and more events took place than had during all of the previous 307 years. (Actually, there had been rumors of gold in many parts as early as 1816, and in 1842 a Francisco Lopez had found it far to the south in San Feliciano Canyon. But there was not enough; the moment of history was not ripe, and little heed was paid to it anywhere, by anyone.)

At first people found the discovery hard to believe. John Sutter did not want to believe it and tried to keep it quiet. But the glitter of gold could not be concealed. Following its discovery by John Marshall at Colma on January 24, 1848, word spread slowly. Some people in the nearby town went up into the foothills in the spring to see what it was all about. By May 29 it was learned in Monterey. No one was too excited, not too believing. By June 12 a straggler arrived with the yellow stuff in his hand. Another soon displayed gold. Indifference changed to excitement. By the end of July hardly a soul was left in Monterey. It was the same from Sonoma to San Diego. Every male rushed to the mountains. Before long several hundred deserted ships formed a forest of naked masts in San Francisco Bay. But some captains did manage to muster crews and sail out the Golden Gate and they carried the news with them. Word spread swiftly around the world. Men packed their belongings and started for California—from the east coast, Europe, Asia, Africa, Australia, the Orient, South America, they came; over land, across the Atlantic, the Pacific, the Isthmus of Panama, around the Horn. The stampede was on.

By the end of 1849 conservative estimates show an increase in population in California from about 20,000 to 100,000. San Francisco numbered 850 souls when the rush began; 12 months later her population was 35,000—and many more had long since passed through on the way to the gold fields, with hordes yet to come.

Chaos reigned for a while, especially since there was no formal government! Bandits roamed El Camino Real. San Francisco and Sacramento were cities of shanties and saloons that burned and rose again many times during the next decade. Up in the foothills of the Sierra, stream banks and gulches that had never felt a white man's foot suddenly became towns with populations of many thousands each and such hastily contrived names as Bedbug, Poker Flat, You Bet, Angels Camp. Men from many places dug, scratched, and sifted the soil, sand, and water. Good men and bad men, good soil and bad soil, good liquor and bad liquor, guns and knives.

In ten short years it was all over, but something big had happened to California. She at last had a population to do something with her tremendous, but heretofore unused, potentialities. Men who had come to seek gold, stayed to build more solid futures in business, farming, shipping, and transportation. California grew.

She became the 31st state on September 9, 1850 and finally settled her capital at Sacramento, having recently moved it from Monterey, to San Jose, to San Francisco, and Benicia.

In the spring of 1854 Theodore Judah arrived with a dream of a different metal—iron, two bands of it that could carry steam engines over mountains and across rivers and plains. His dream was even too fantastic for the visionary, gambling men of California. He finally trimmed his sails and talked only in local terms, of the profits to be made from hauling goods to the now booming silver mines in Nevada. In Sacramento, four men listened to him and lifted their eyes beyond their separate and mundane occupations of groceries, dry goods, and hardware. Leland Stanford, Charles Crocker, Mark Hopkins, and Collis Huntington soon found themselves in the business of building a great railroad—how great they had no idea at the time.

Federal funds and ambitions soon entered the picture. A railroad from east to west! Judah's dream, and the dream of millions, but not of his partners, The Big Four, who were more interested in a short line to the mines. Judah lost out to his partners, and returned to New York and died shortly after. The Big Four went on with their Central Pacific Railroad, literally making millions by the mile as they formed their own separate subcontract companies to drain off the construction profits to be had with both government and people anxious to invest in the great dream. The Big Four carried through —through miles of solid granite, over vast chasms, around lofty peaks, rushing rivers and deserts to meet the Union Pacific on May 10, 1869 and drive the gold spike that at last joined east and west— and really opened up California!

But the masses did not rush to buy tickets to California. The rates were too high and the time was not yet ripe. Apathy held back the easterners. Grant was president and Boss Tweed reigned scandalously. Business was bad everywhere. The Bank of California collapsed as did many eastern organizations. Only the wealthy came, but they arrived in sufficient numbers to fill the fabulous and luxurious hotels that sprang up—The Arlington at Santa Barbara, the Del Monte near Monterey, the Raymond in Pasadena, The Coronado near San Diego, and others. With San Francisco and Los Angeles connected by rail in 1876, the wealthy could travel up and down the state in style.

San Francisco was still an ugly city, known as one of the dirtiest in the world because of the constant soot given off by the smoke from very low grade western soft coal. Yet, she was proud of her new hostelries— The Palace being her greatest claim to international fame. Within a very few years the earthquake of 1906 would shake her badly and start fires that would burn her out. From it she quickly rose to international fame as one of the most beautiful of all cities, her white buildings constantly cleaned by the almost nightly fogs, her air lacking soot because of the change from coal to natural gas as a more economical means of heat.

Culture came to California, the new kind, the 20th century kind, to replace the void of the previous two decades when men had too much else to do. Most of it started in the north, especially in San Francisco. Universities, libraries, opera houses, and theaters grew rapidly. Clubs were dedicated to the arts and literature. During this period Robert Louis Stevenson in Monterey and Henry George and Jack London in San Francisco were writing books that are still in print today.

Los Angeles was far behind, still a little, sleepy town. The gold rush had passed her by to plunge straight through San Francisco. But a new kind of rush for a different but wealth-producing gold was about to hit her hard.

In 1881 a new rail link, the Southern Pacific, was forged from Los Angeles to the Deep South. Four years later the Santa Fe Railway started trains over new tracks from Chicago to Los Angeles. A price war started—and so did the passengers. By the end of 1886 the price of a ticket from Kansas City to Los Angeles was down from $ 125 to $ 25; then to $ 18.00, to $ 8.00, and finally to screaming advertisements—"Kansas City to Los Angeles—$ 1.00. Why not take a look? Only a dollar." Interesting trip—and a lot of people had been talking for a long time about the glories of California. Into Los Angeles they poured, eight to ten train loads every day in the winter of 1887—to be met at the station by promoters filled with wonderful ideas on how to make a fortune at once and live even more confortably in the salubrious climate. In three years many an acre increased from less than $ 100 to $ 3,000 and was then promptly broken into six lots which sold for $ 2,500 each. One fast-talking speculator bought 3,000 lots in the nearby Mojave Desert for about 15 cents each and sold them for $ 250 apiece.

Mixed with all of this land boom was a most inviting form of gold—the gold of lush, easily grown oranges. It would be very pleasant to sit in the California sun and reap a fortune from a few acres of golden oranges which were so easy to grow. Best of all, two kinds grew and produced fruit at different times of the year, permitting the grower to count on a continuous harvest, and the transcontinental railroads provided an easily and profitably reached market.

The bubble burst, of course; but Los Angeles was on its way at last with a population of 50,000 enjoying its balmy climate in 1892. The City of the Angels quickly began to make up for lost time. Several colleges and libraries were founded that are now recognized as centers of learning. Discovery of oil at the turn of the century attracted industrial growth; the opening of harbor facilities at San Pedro brought world trade; and international interest began to focus on the locality as an entertainment center after Hollywood stepped into the spotlight. The city has grown with unparalleled speed: for six decades after 1870 it doubled in population every census period. Today, this great sprawling metropolis, third largest city in the nation, is an industrial giant and, because of its many attractions and pleasant climate, a powerful magnet for tourists.

In 1890, California was still sparsely settled even with a population of 1,200,000, and the railroads needed customers to keep the wheels rolling over their thousands of miles of shiny new track. Advertisements extolling the glories of California appeared in eastern newspapers. Glowing handbills found their way into thousands of eastern cities, hamlets, and crossroads. The Southern Pacific Railroad founded a very successful publication in 1898, named *Sunset Magazine*, with eastern distribution as its goal. Within 20 years it was no longer necessary to promote California. *Sunset* was transformed into a literary journal to serve the growing population in California and her sister states which were also developing rapidly during this period. In 1928, *Sunset* was acquired by its present owners and became a magazine for Westerners only.

But still the people came. The move was on. The gold had started it, the rush to Los Angeles had added fuel to the fire; man's natural desire to move ever westward was still strong. California continued to be a mecca for many in far places. The dream first given a name by Montalvo more than four centuries ago still worked its magic.

Today they are still coming. In 1920, California counted 3,500,000 residents; in 1940 it was nearly 7,000,000. Now it is well over 13,000,000, and the experts predict more than 20,000,000 by 1970. It is now second only to New York State and many predictions show it as the number one state by 1965.

That is the story of the people who have come to California during the four centuries since Rodriguez Cabrillo, the Portuguese, first stepped on her soil. These are the people who have built the buildings, the roads, the bridges, the dams; who planted the orange, and lemon and walnut and apricot; who brought the grapes and developed her famed wines; who tapped great underground seas of oil; who brought the eucalyptus that trademarks her many highways, the cattle that move on her hills, the miles upon miles of cotton and corn, tobacco and lettuce, avocado and artichoke.

Karl Obert's beautiful pictures reflect all of this as it reveals man's small marks on the grandeur that is natural California, one part of the world that is too vastly varied to create any one impression upon visitors. Her 1,200 miles of rocky coast hold back the blue Pacific, dotted here and there with sandy beaches and coves. Her tree-clad mountains match her softly rounded hills that are gold in summer and green in spring. Her hundreds of valleys run mostly north and south through the Coast Range along the ocean, and the greatest valley of them all, the San Joaquin, lies between her two great ranges and reaches 400 miles from the Cascades in the north to the Tehachapi near Los Angeles. Many of her redwood trees have pointed steadily toward her blue skies for more than two thousand years. The snow-capped granite peaks of her High Sierra create sharp and close contrast to her great deserts that attract thousands every winter. The granite walls of her incomparable, cathedral-like Yosemite will never show any evidence of man's presence.

This is California.

Editor

Index of Pictures

Apple Valley 191
Avalon Bay, Catalina Island 50

Berkeley 130, 131
Big Bear Lake 184
Bodie 230, 231
Buena Park 47

Cactus 192
Carmel 99, 101–104
Carson Pass 232
Castle Crag 149
Catalina Island 50
Cattle Ranch 44
Coachella Valley 187
Columbia 160–163
Convict Lake 215
Coronado 34

Death Valley 194, 196, 197, 199–201, 203
Deer 145
Desert Cactus 192
Desert Hot Springs 188
Desert Palms 186, 187, 193
Devils Postpile National Monument 222, 223, 226

Disneyland 41–43, 46
Donner Lake. 236, 237
Donner Monument 239
Donner Pass 236

Elk 144
Eucalyptus Trees 94

Fiesta, Santa Barbara 82, 84, 85
Fort Bragg 142
Fort Ross 143

Gaviota Pass 93
Golden Gate Bridge. 128

Hume Lake 176

Jackson 158
Joshua Trees 182, 183, 190, 191
June Lake 225

Klammath River 146
Knott's Berry Farm 47

La Jolla 35
Lake Tahoe 233–235
Long Beach 52–55
Los Angeles 56–70

Mammoth Lakes 214, 216–219
Mammoth Mountain 221
Marin County 132
Mendocino County 141, 142
Midway Point 102
Minarets 213
Missions:
    Dolores, San Francisco 115
    San Antonio 96
    San Carlos 99, 101

San Diego de Alcala 27
San Juan Bautista 106
San Juan Capistrano 38, 39
San Luis Rey 37
San Miguel 97
Santa Barbara 84, 86, 89
Santa Ines 87, 88
Sonoma 133
Mojave Desert 182, 183, 185, 190, 191, 198
Mojave River 185
Montecito 72, 77–81, 83
Monterey 100, 105
Monterey Cypress 102, 103
Mother Lode Country 158, 160–165
Mount Lassen 154, 155
Mount Palomar 40
Mount Shasta 148, 153
Mount Whitney 204, 205

Oil Wells 54, 55, 73

Pala 36
Palm Canyon 193
Palm Springs 189, 193
Palo Alto 108–111
Palomar Observatory 40
Palos Verdes 48, 49, 51
Pinnacles National Monument 98
Point Loma 31

Rancheros Visitadores 90, 91
Redwoods 140
Richmond 134
Rock Creek Lake 210
Russian River 136, 137

Sacramento 156, 157, 159
Salton Sea 195

San Antonio Mission 96
San Bernardino Mountains 184
San Diego 25, 26, 27, 29–33
San Francisco 112–129
San Francisco Bay 126, 128, 129, 135
San Francisco-Oakland Bay Bridge 129
San Gabriel Valley 45
San Juan Bautista 106, 107
San Juan Capistrano 38, 39
San Luis Rey 37
San Marino 71
San Miguel 97
Santa Barbara 74–76, 82, 84–86, 89, 92
Santa Ynez Valley 87, 88, 90, 91
Scotty's Castle 199, 201, 203
Seacliff 73
Sequoia National Park 176, 178, 180, 181
Shadow Lake 227
Shasta Dam 151
Shasta Lake 150–152
Sherwin Grade 211
Sierra Nevada Mountains 202, 204–229, 232–239
Signal Hill 54, 55
Solvang 87, 88
Sonoma 133
Sonoma County 136, 137, 138, 139, 143
Stanford University 108–111
State Capitol Building 156

Tioga Pass 220
Trinity River 147

University of California at Berkeley 130, 131
University of California at Los Angeles 68, 69

Yosemite National Park 166–175, 177, 179
Yucca 95

California Tower, Balboa Park, San Diego

San Diego, Civic Center

Mission San Diego de Alcala

San Diego Waterfront

Sunset on San Diego Bay

Façade in Balboa Park, San Diego

Lighthouse, Cabrillo National Monument, Point Loma

Museum of Man, Balboa Park

The Fine Arts Gallery, Balboa Park

Hotel del Coronado, Coronado

Seashore at La Jolla

Cemetery at Pala Mission, Indian Reservation

Mission San Luis Rey

Corridor at Mission San Juan Capistrano

Patio and Bells at Capistrano

Mount Palomar Observatory with largest telescope in the world, 200 inches

41   Side view of Fairytale Castle, Disneyland, near Anaheim

Fairytale Castle, Disneyland

Rocket to the Moon in Tomorrowland, Disneyland

Cattle Ranch, San Diego County

Orange Grove in San Gabriel Valley

Santa Clara County Free Library
San Jose, Calif.

Boat Landing in Adventureland, Disneyland

Restored Ghost Town, Knott's Berry Farm, Buena Park

Wayfarer's Chapel, Palos Verdes

Cities by the Sea from Palos Verdes

Avalon Bay, Catalina Island

Shoreline at Palos Verdes

Long Beach

Amusement Park, Long Beach

Signal Hill near Long Beach

View of Long Beach from Signal Hill

Los Angeles City Hall

Pershing Square, Los Angeles

Mexican Market, Olvera Street, Los Angeles

Olvera Street, Los Angeles

Apartment Houses, Los Angeles

MacArthur Park, Los Angeles

Chinatown, Los Angeles

Los Angeles Library

Wilshire Boulevard, Los Angeles

Modern Buildings on Wilshire Boulevard, Los Angeles

Mausoleum at Forest Lawn, Los Angeles

Hall of the Crucifixion, Forest Lawn Cemetery, Los Angeles

Royce Hall, University of California (U. C. L. A.), Los Angeles

Santa Clara County Free Library
San Jose, Calif.

69

Library, U. C. L. A.

Biltmore Hotel, Los Angeles

Henry E. Huntington Memorial Library and Art Gallery, San Marino

Pacific Shoreline, Montecito

Oil Wells at Seacliff

Along the Boulevard in Santa Barbara

Santa Barbara County Courthouse

On the Edge of the Pacific, Santa Barbara

Channel Drive in Montecito

Formal Garden, Montecito

Mediterranean Mansion, Montecito

Entrance to Graholm, Montecito Estate

Interior of Graholm

Old Spanish Days Fiesta, Santa Barbara

Overlooking the Blue Pacific

Spanish Serenade, Santa Barbara

Flower Girl, Fiesta Time, Santa Barbara

Mission Santa Barbara "Queen of the Missions"

Mission Santa Ines, Solvang

Ruins of the Past (Santa Ines Mission)

Monastery Shadows (Santa Barbara Mission)

Los Rancheros Visitadores (RV), Santa Ynez Valley

River Crossing (RV)

In the Foothills of Santa Barbara

Historic Gaviota Pass

Three Brothers, Eucalyptus Trees

"Candle of the Lord", Wild Yucca

Arches of San Antonio Mission

Mission San Miguel

Pinnacles National Monument

Bell Tower of Mission San Carlos, Carmel

Royal Presidio Chapel, Monterey

Mission San Carlos Borromeo, Carmel

Midway Point, Carmel Bay

Windswept Cypress, 17-Mile Drive

Carmel Shoreline

Fishing Fleet, Monterey

Mission San Juan Bautista

Old Castro House, San Juan Bautista

Stanford University at Palo Alto

Library at Stanford

Courtyard at Stanford

Stanford Memorial Chapel

Monument of Francis Scott Key, composer of "The Star-Spangled Banner", San Francisco

Civic Center, San Francisco

Palace of Fine Arts, San Francisco

Mission Dolores, San Francisco

San Francisco Ferry Building

Church of St. Peter and St. Paul

San Francisco Skyline

Santa Clara County Free Library
San Jose, Calif.

119   San Francisco at night — with Oakland and Berkeley across the Bay (Joseph-Muench-Photo)

Chinatown, San Francisco

Financial District, San Francisco

Botanic Garden, Golden Gate Park, San Francisco

De Young Museum, Golden Gate Park, San Francisco

Japanese Garden, Golden Gate Park

Japanese Gateway, Golden Gate Park

Fog Entering San Francisco Bay

Fisherman's Wharf, San Francisco

Golden Gate Bridge

San Francisco-Oakland Bay Bridge

Campus, University of California, Berkeley

Zoology and Botany Building, University of California, Berkeley

St. Vincent's Boys' School, Marin County

Mission in Sonoma

Night Scene, Richmond Refinery, Standard Oil Company of California

Santa Clara County Free Library
San Jose, Calif.

Richmond—San Rafael Ferry

Russian River near Guerneville

Along the Russian River

Prune Orchard near Healdsburg

Vineyard in Sonoma County

Redwood Highway U.S. 101 near Eureka

Coastline near Elk, Mendocino County

Sawmill in Fort Bragg

Russian Orthodox Chapel, Fort Ross, State Historical Monument

Elk, Northern California

Deer in Velvet, Northern California

Martin's Ferry, Klammath River

Tranquil Trinity River

Mount Shasta from Sacramento River

Castle Crag

Shimmering Shasta Lake

Shasta Dam, largest in California

Boat Landing on Shasta Lake

Mount Shasta

Mount Lassen from Reflection Lake

154

Lassen Peak Highway

State Capitol, Sacramento

State Office Building, Sacramento

Tailing Wheels, in the Gold Rush Country, near Jackson

Sutter's Fort, Sacramento

Old Red Brick Schoolhouse in Columbia

Santa Clara County Free Library
San Jose, Calif.

161

Fallon House Theater, Columbia

Wells Fargo Express Office in Old Columbia

St. Anna's Church, Columbia

Moccasin Creek Power House

Mother Lode Country near Mariposa

Merced River, Yosemite National Park

Yosemite National Park, El Capitan and Three Brothers

Mirror Lake, Yosemite

Half Dome, Yosemite

Winter in Yosemite

El Capitan, Yosemite

Vernal Falls, Yosemite

Yosemite Falls

Big Trees, Mariposa Grove

Little Church, Yosemite

Hume Lake near Sequoia National Park

Skiing at Badger Pass, Yosemite

Among the Giant Sequoias, Sequoia National Park

Tunnel Tree, Mariposa Grove, Yosemite

Giant Sequoias

Morro Rock, Sequoia National Park

Sunset on the Desert, Apple Valley

Winter in the Mojave Desert near Palmdale

Big Bear Lake, San Bernardino Mountains

Mojave River near Victorville

Desert Palms

Date Palms, Coachella Valley

Cabot's Old Indian Pueblo, Desert Hot Springs

El Mirador, Palm Springs

Desert Meditation, showing San Bernardino Mountain Range

Joshua Trees, Apple Valley

Cactus in Bloom

Native Palms, Palm Canyon

Santa Clara County Free Library
San Jose, Calif.

Morning on the Desert

Boiling Mud Pots, Salton Sea

Sand Dunes in Death Valley

Wandering Hills

Rock Formation in the Desert

Death Valley, Scotty's Castle

Natural Bridge, Death Valley

Scotty's Castle

Grazing Pack Mules, High Sierra

Panamint Mountains from Scotty's Castle

View of Mount Whitney near Lone Pine

Sierra Nevada and Mount Whitney from Alabama Hills

Desert Mystery

The High Sierra, North of Bishop

Cattle near Bishop

Sierra Vista

Rock Creek Lake

View from Sherwin Grade looking South

Approaching Storm, near Convict Lake

The Minarets

Twin Lakes, Mammoth Lakes

Fishing Boats, Convict Lake

Tranquil Lake Mary

Santa Clara County Free Library
San ____, Calif.

Boat Landing, Lake Mary

Lake Mamie, Mammoth Lakes

Horseshoe Lake, Mammoth Lakes

Looking West Toward Tioga Pass

Mammoth Mountain

Devils Postpile National Monument

June Lake in January

View from Reds Meadows, Devils Postpile

Shadow Lake

Winter Fantasy

Sunset in the High Sierra

Ghost Town of Bodie

Old Church in Bodie

Sheep near Carson Pass

Emerald Bay, Lake Tahoe

Lake Tahoe

Pine-studden Shoreline, Lake Tahoe

Donner Pass and Lake

Donner Lake

Sentinel of Donner Pass

The inscription on the monument reads:

VIRILE TO RISE AND
FIND; KINDLY WITHAL
AND A READY HELP.
FACING THE BRUNT
OF FATE; INDOMI-
TABLE,—UNAFRAID.